ALSO BY JULIAN LYNN

Four Gates to Health

Yoga's Devotional Light

Divine Fruit
Ecstatic Verse

Julian Lynn

Nymphaea Works · Springfield, Missouri

Divine Fruit

Ecstatic Verse

Copyright © 2014 by Julian Lynn

All rights reserved.

Published in the United States by Nymphaea Works.

Library of Congress Cataloging-in-Publication Data
Lynn, Julian
Divine fruit: ecstatic verse / Julian Lynn. –1st ed.

ISBN 978-0-578-13234-1

1. Devotional literature. 2. Devotional poetry, American.
3. American poetry—women authors.
I. Lynn, Julian. II. Title

2013920540

Dewey-Decimal-System Classification: 811

A selection of work in this book first appeared in the title, *Plastic and Red Hot: A Collection of Devotional Work*.

For permissions, please contact questions@julianlynn.com

The written and photographic works contained in this book are protected by copyright. Please do not reproduce, transmit, perform or store by any means—electronic or mechanical—whether in part or in whole, excepting brief excerpts for purposes of review, any of the work contained herein without the written permission of the author/photographer.

ISBN: 978-0-578-13234-1

To the Grace and Light That is God.

PREFACE

As a child, I was untutored in the skills required to uncover and articulate the longings of my heart. Over the years, I found myself becoming increasingly frustrated with an unnamed and unsatisfied desire. In adulthood, I sometimes felt mapless, as though I were opening and closing an endless series of doors on scenes and situations—some of which I would rather not have experienced. Who was I? Where was I going?

Then, I became physically ill. In my physical sickness and the tiredness of my heart, I packed my bags mentally with all of my belongings. And, not knowing where or how God might come for me, by train or by bus, I would alternate my daily routine of waiting in my mind's eye between the two most likely locations—depot and station.

But God did not come as I had anticipated—as a discrete entity in a quiet cloud to grant me release from the pain in my body. Instead, the Face of God came in a myriad of forms and persons holding the keys to my being and becoming.

This book, then, is created from a seat of devotion and in gratitude toward the Divine Creative Force—Supreme Grace—with a humble devotion for and toward God. I am grateful for being granted another chance at uncovering the desires of my heart. And, I am especially grateful for my experiences of Union. It is in this spirit that I offer this book to you, to celebrate your own moments of connectedness and the purity in your own true heart, in the hopes that we may all expand our experiences of Oneness.

Julian Lynn
Fall, 2013

TABLE OF CONTENTS

Divine Fruit	....	1
Out Loud	....	2
Quiet	....	3
While Napping	....	4
Meditation	....	5
Know Love	....	6
1,000 Blossoms	....	7
Rank	....	8
Spring Green	....	9
Asunder	....	10
Seamlessly	....	11
Unbridled	....	12

Underbelly	....	13
Spark of Life	....	14
Fool	....	15
Gifts	....	16
Liberation	....	17
Full	....	18
Remaining	....	19
Chant	....	20
Flow	....	21
On That Sweet Final Day	....	22
Endless	....	23
Desire	....	24
Pine Cone	....	25
Nakedness	....	26
Rabid	....	27
Progress	....	28
Elegant and Concise	....	30
Grammar	....	31
Essential Self	....	32
Holy Matchstick	....	33
Salt Water	....	34
Plastic and Red Hot...	....	35
Most Pleasing	....	36

Twice More	....	38
Calling Cards	....	39
Promise	....	40
Midnight Sky	....	41
Sidewalks	....	42
Sliced Lemon/Crushed Mint	....	43
Sun Streamers	....	44
Daily Bread	....	45
As Lichens	....	46
Hearts	....	47
Falling	....	48
A Letter from the Sun	....	49
Sacred	....	50
New Poem II	....	51
Parchment	....	52
Ripeness	....	53
Into Pyrex	....	54
Vibrant	....	55
Utterance	....	56
Appendix	....	59
Index	....	65
Grace	....	72

Ecstatic Verse

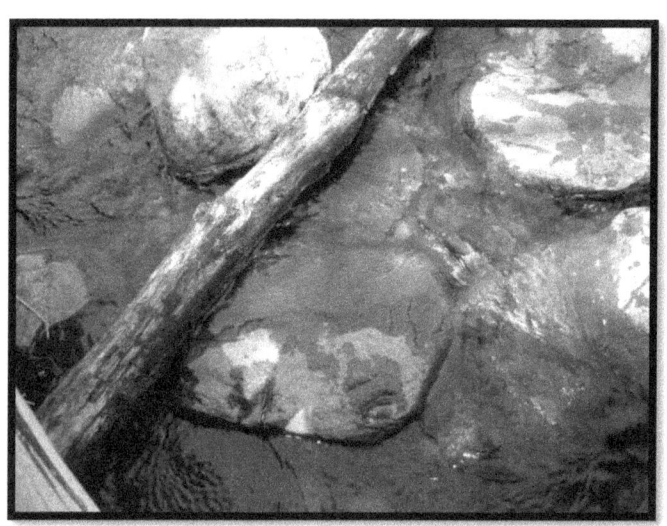

DIVINE FRUIT

Once the fruit
of Divine offering
has been tasted,
there is no other.

OUT LOUD

───────────────────────

I want to touch You
The way You embraced me.
"Then you had better get to singing lusty songs
Of true celebration and thanksgiving."

In gratitude, I want to tangle myself in You
For all of the sensual kisses You granted me.
"Then set your belly on the bed and write
Those letters of gratitude to strangers and friends."

I want to curl up next to You
In the manner You ensconced me when I was in need.
"Child, pack your pockets full of dried fruits,
Canned tuna, sardines and sealed saltines,
So the next beggar I send to your attention can eat."

I want to remember You always
The way You never forget me.
"Turn the strength and ability of your full heart
On the most difficult of Divine requests,
And we can wrestle them together."

Julian Lynn

I want to grow tendrils to protect You in gratitude
For the way You came to enliven my dying body.
"Place your words like soft, clean dressings
On the scarred and wounded returning from war."

I want to place my forehead on the floor, hands resting
On Your feet—just as You honored my fragile frame.
"Remember always that every physical vessel
Is a holy body full of My Sacred Light."

QUIET
_____

Still me.

Divine Fruit

WHILE NAPPING
_____

One day,
Plants came to grow
On all of the compost
Cradled in my hips—
Waste shovelled there
By the who, what and where
Of many years of living.

Digging deep, into the overripe
Soil of my experience,
I thanked God
For the Mercy of those white roots—
Able to convert my overfull bucket
Into something: Green,
Alive, Beautiful.

Breaking into my fouled
And fractured bones,
God's touch bound me
Side to side, top to bottom
Repairing my vessel.

Mercy, secure me.

MEDITATION

How do you tell a man—
God has moved in my body.

Smile at me—glance, gaze,
wish what you will.

That tender, fertile ground
is all planted.

Peer—not.

My physicality—
all sown up.

Though the gate is closed,
I will not leave you without hope.

At your request,
your hands, mind, body, Soul
come into Stillness.

I'll share
the pass key.

Divine Fruit

KNOW LOVE

_____

God's Grace tickled your toes.
Then, with a snort,
Laughter burbled from your nose.

Soft rolling baby feet
Perched on my seat.
Doughy arms, dimpled knees—
Stand you up tall please.

Shine and smile and laugh.
Burst radiant into this world.

1,000 BLOSSOMS

If I were to gather 1,000 blossoms in a basket,
they would not be brilliant enough.

If I were to prepare confectioner's chocolates
and bring them wrapped in satin boxes,
they would not be fine enough.

If I were to cradle You in a downy blue blanket,
humming an endless and inaudible lullaby,
it would not be subtle enough.

No color, texture, sound
or fragrance—
nothing
for all of my gratitude.

Divine Fruit

RANK

_____

Leave me—you crusty demon,
Virulent oaf—wanting to infiltrate and infect
Every cell in my body with wayward thoughts
And greedy, self-serving ways.

Somehow, I woke up next to you this morning.
While my eyes were still closed,
Your breath tipped me off
To the fact that I was not alone.
Then, I felt the dry sweat crunch
In the bristly hairs of your body
And wondered what I had done
To invite *you* into my bed.

Ah, it was that uncharitable thought
I had last night
That came from the seeping, abraded
Pit of an old injury.
It must have reopened at the party.
Best I should head to the doctor
And have that wound cauterized than
Suffer one more day highjacked
By the crust of your presence.

SPRING GREEN
───────────────

Heave up
the soil.
Push brokenness
aside.
Cut through
the lot.
Green blade
growing.

Divine Fruit

ASUNDER
_____

Shatter asunder
all that remains
of my fixed heart
against You.

I will go.

Bow gently
to comb the rubble.
Press Your breath
into the embers.

I will burn.

I almost died
waiting for You.

Cast me,
reignited,
into the where
of Your willing.

I will fly.

SEAMLESSLY

I hold You
in all of that and those
put into my hands—
realizing Your touch.

UNBRIDLED

That day—
kicking and snorting
impossible
to stand still,
waiting for the bell
in that starting gate of confinement—
rocking with tremors
and haunches flexed.

Quell your desire
to complete the course
in the starting gate.
A strong finish comes
in the pastures of your maturity—
in caring for the fellow Soul
of an innocent.

UNDERBELLY
_____

My preconditioned
Responses
Are not working
Today.

I play the Whore,
The Accommodator, the Pleaser,
The Bully, when in full retort,
And go home—
Tail between my legs,
Head hung low,
Ears flat back.

Soul, Arise!

Shine in my body;
So that, when I turn
On the flat of my back at night,
Safe at home,
The warm hand of God may
Comfort the skin of my underbelly.

SPARK OF LIFE

_____

When Michelangelo's God
extended his hand to Adam
and—with the touch of His finger—
imbued Adam with life,
He did not know
what would ensue.

Adam—upon descent—
embraced his earthy
commanding self.
I am this.
You are that.
We are not.

And then,
in the Fall,
Adam remembered
the Grace of that first touch;
and, lifting his whole heart
to heaven,
he extended all of himself
to Divine Creation.

Why in my seeking is there
grief?

Open your heart. And grieve
the pain of our long separation.

FOOL
_____

Lover,
I sent you away.

Divine Fruit

GIFTS

Do not bestow
Upon me that which
I do not already possess—
The scent and color
Of Your own Purity.

LIBERATION

_____

Waiting to hear the death rattle
of my own false self—
wrap that petty idol
in burial vestments.

Lay it to rest.
Sleep.
Sleep.

Waking one morning
to hear the squall
and demands
of a newborn.

Bring on the daylight.
Wake.
Wake.

Fierce sun, wind piercing—
one life
swept up
Liberation come.

FULL
_____

Remake my bones

Into a bottomless pit

Of cordwood

So that by crumpled newsprint,

By stick,

By split log—

I may furnish barren hearts with

Fodder for their empty hearths.

Light of God,

Wind at my back;

Emblazon us all.

REMAINING
_____

My heart
may fly away,
but my joy will remain.

Divine Fruit

CHANT

When I whisper in your ear
the many Names
of God,
I perceive your mouth curling
into a smile
and your once dormant heart
shimmering with the Sound.

The shaking in your Soul
tells me that
your body knows
Union
primordial
with the One
true Tone of
the only Name.

FLOW
_____

Turning to me,
the River asked,
Which way should
we go?

Walking into
churning waters,
extending my trust,
I answered,
You know.

Entwined,
we were there.

ON THAT SWEET FINAL DAY

On that sweet final day,
visit me
in my garden;
lay me down
among the flowers
in that freshly turned soil.
I will not deny You access
to my body.

When the cherubs sing,
it will be a visit
from the butterflies and
hummingbirds,
sipping nectar
near the unbound wings
of my Soul.

ENDLESS

Night came to settle.
Day rose.
Rhythm mine
Match this endless
Parade.

DESIRE
_____

How can I love them—
When my mind jeers,
"Stodgy old farts!"
After they tell me their "preferences"
And reveal that the folds
Of their grey matter have become
A stagnant, unsolvable maze?

How can I love them as they are—
When the words that fall
From their lips and
Pinch their tongues
Scuttle from their throats
And their burnt-up hearts,
Professing doubt about
You and me
And the Godhead within?

Patient as ever, You tell me,
"Love them anyway."

And I have to crumble at that command

Because—in the end—
I too am stodgy and old
Spending days sometimes
Locked in the confines of
My own mind
Only to be freed
By the careful touch of
Your unflagging Desire—
To be shown how to Love again.

PINE CONE

Fire, come;
crack me open.

NAKEDNESS
___

Let me dwell in Your nakedness.
Others may clothe You,
shunning Your brilliance,
shocked by Your radiance.

Open a door to me,
and I will wait.
I am raw with waiting.
Enfold me in Your nakedness.

Almost hidden to me,
You passed under my window
in the cobbled garb of sectarians.
Come up
into the room
and it will be ours—
to strip away
false layers.

Saturate me
and purge our separateness.
I know You to be everywhere.

RABID

_____

My Soul contorted
with the ugly words
coming from my mouth.
My Friend said,
"It looks like a rabid dog
bit you. Come now—
with this poker,
hot from the fire,
I will sear
the wound in your heart."

PROGRESS
_____

I want to halt this process—
stop progress—
in its tracks.
I want to choose
another clichéd existence
to dismantle,
to select another
reel
to unwind.

No viewing necessary.
No sorrow.
No shame.
No doubt.

No more responsibility,
not from me,
never.

Take your bag of collected skulls
and set those Souls free.

Almighty God, forgive me.

Chant, sing, drum...
hum—God.
God be here.
God be with me.
God help.

Have I really been so?

Move over Bluebeard.
I have opened the closet.
I will chant you down
to finish the job,
holding your knife
to my own throat.

Peace to you.

ELEGANT AND CONCISE

She whispered,
"Who are you?"

From that expanded cradle of Stillness—
Heavy morning mist;
Turned earth;
Crisp linens;
Aromatic tea;
She said,
"I smell heaven."

GRAMMAR

Speak—
what would you
say...
unfettered by language,
unhindered by grammar,
limiting constructs unknown?

Rigid rules are removed.

Love move
into me.

Hot rise of wonder
rest for a moment.

ESSENTIAL SELF

_____

I belched black today.
It was the black crust
that held my fixed
ego in place.

And then there was
the loosening.
The loosening
of ton after load
after pound after avalanche
of all my notions
about who I wanted to be.

This grounding in reality,
without whim or holy fantasy
to bear me aloft, is cold—
to say the least.

Stuck so long
in the ice cube
of my own personal hell—
immobile—as Dante's three.

"And whom have I betrayed?"
I ask,
as a dark vapor
leaves my cavernous heart.

The Self.

HOLY MATCHSTICK

Ignite the coals.
Cold heart set on fire.

SALT WATER
_____

Whoever, whatever

Made me think

That I was other than You?

Whatever, whoever

Made me

Close my heart?

Whoever, whatever

Said that

We were not One?

Drench me.

PLASTIC AND RED HOT...

Plastic and red hot,
You took me from the fire—
resting, striking, turning me
on the anvil.

You twisted my new shape
and forged me a new curve;
the idol
of my rigid form
was broken.

Quench me in the water.

From my nascent cooling body,
vapors from archaic patterns
dissipate.

MOST PLEASING

───────────────────

Let me do the things
most pleasing to You
while I occupy this body.

Let me bring laughter
to over-dry faces and spritz them
with the moisture of mirth so that
when they howl and guffaw for the first time—
since only You know when—their cheeks
won't crack with the burden of Joy.

Let me breeze between the bodies of two
puffed up and enraged roosters—
ready to wing-beat and peck each other
to death. May Your Grace
cause them to scratch their heads
and forget their plans
for violence and pain.

Let me grow calm and steady—
as I prepare to run

with my hand on
the back of a bicycle seat—
assisting one of Your children
as they set their fulcrum squarely
within the state of Your balance.

Let me love the crazy circus
of misfits and injured—
even as we trip ourselves and others—
in search of the comfort
only You can provide.

Let me forgive
those rogue protectors
of all that is rigid, selfish,
unkind and blindly ignorant,
while I trust You to speak
to our hearts of Oneness.

TWICE MORE

―――――――――――――

When Zeus showered Danaë
with the gold coins of his love,
she opened her royal loins—
expanding her dress
with the strength of her thighs—
to catch all of him
in the full force of his decent.

That first early morning—
upon waking—
dazed and smothered,
I saw You out
and locked
the door.
Under the intensity of Your intentions,
I collapsed.

The emptiness in my fragile body
did not leave—
the longing ceaseless—
until You visited
twice more.

CALLING CARDS

"Let Love return to your house."
I was told one overly serious afternoon
on the heels of seven days of sorrow.

"Where is your delight in the day?"
I was asked after failing to see
the sun winking and smiling—my head
bent by a dreadful kink in my neck.

"You have forgotten the hidden treasures
I tucked away for you in each day.
I will send you a map to jog your memory,
so you can hunt for some fun."

"Is there anything else I can do?"
inquired Supreme Grace.
"You have put off answering My calling cards."

And, with that, my eyes opened,
my head lifted, and I saw the stack—
and marveled at the patience of my Friend
waiting for my return.

Divine Fruit

PROMISE

It began,
show and tell
hide and seek
truth or dare.

We played
for seasons on end
in all locations
in all manner
of weather.

You afforded me
respite—
taking mercifully
to the clouds.

I am tired.

These past days
have been cloudless;
and, I am worn thin.

A night
engagement?

The moon shines
as a promise.

MIDNIGHT SKY
_____

Heaven
is in your Soul.

SIDEWALKS

I moved as a Bishop today
across the sidewalk-tiled board.
Gliding, I moved among Souls,
old and gilded
young and ugly
beauty unpolished—
unspoken.

Diagonally, I moved among
a mixed set of pieces,
scattered, collected and matched
to play.
Gallop, retreat, capture,
hide, shield.

Some charge in chase
down side alleyways.

I moved in
to talk to a King,
fronted by three Pawns.

He turned in terror,

fleeing one space,

feeling trapped and had,

never realizing the luster

and strength of his own crown.

SLICED LEMON / CRUSHED MINT
_____

The fragrance

of God's Realm

Spilled over

Into the glory of the day.

SUN STREAMERS
_____

Laughing Sun,
Stop teasing me.

I have told You—no—
Before.
And, again—
My hair comes undone;
My blouse damp,
Unbuttoned;
And Your heat
From the black asphalt
Shines under
My skirt.

Without You tonight,
How can I be complete?

DAILY BREAD

Upon waking,
share hot, buttered toast
with a four-legged Friend.
Later, scatter tidbits from
a mid-morning pastry
in the park.
Bow to Squirrels and Birds.
Next, cast your change
into the yawning, velvety body
of a Musician's case.
Remain to applaud.
It is an exchange of wavelengths.
In the early evening,
with a new-found, hungry Friend,
halve a sandwich.
When you are safely home
and your shoes are by the door,
trust your hot-buttered Friend
to greet you and wipe away
all of the day's mishaps, confusions and
misunderstandings with the simple
broad gestures of an epic tail.
This recipe serves: Many.

Divine Fruit

AS LICHENS

Lying on the cool side
of the damp, grey
rock,
creeping with the soft.
delicate toes of a doily,
we breath together
slowly, imperceptibly
like two white-haired
Lovers.

You wouldn't know
we weren't One.

Julian Lynn

HEARTS

We are—
in the end—
but a fabric
of hearts.

Let us find that place
when we meet—
where warp and weft
coincide.

Let that junction of our coincidence
cause our discourse
to come as from
One tongue.

And although we lie
perpendicular
on the Weaver's loom,
let us strengthen one another and
stand whole as neighbors—
the weakness of our
singularity falling away
with Divine Union.

FALLING

_____

The fissured earth
yielded to
the falling rain.

Fragrances
permeated
my senses,
lifting
alive
immortal
from the soil
underneath
my feet.

Bury me
deeply.

A LETTER FROM THE SUN
_____

I kissed you
a thousand times
or more in our
first three years
together.
We wove a dance
through the trees of the forest—
rays of light,
threads of stability—
supporting you as you moved
among the time-weathered giants
through the trunks of the trees.
You fell quiet,
past an afternoon of laughter,
to nap among the mosses and lichens—
British Soldiers standing guard.
And I, ever vigilant from above,
broke through the leaves of the trees
and the needles of the pines
to guard your crown and
warm the soles of your upturned feet—
sealing your Perfection.

SACRED

_____

You chase the sacred—
some days—
like an end point,
destination, trophy or game.
Your holiness flaps
in the wind like a
soot-soaked battle standard
buffeted about by the wind.
How many knots per hour
do you think you can fly, angel?
Do you plan to hold your
flame steady in a tornado?
End the attempted stillness
and gather your strength instead
to send the arrows of pure action
headlong into the wind—
backed by the steady hand
of Sophia.

NEW POEM II

Most Holy Child,
Aspect of Divine Creation
and God.

May we be forgiven.

Divine Fruit

PARCHMENT

I had to close my eyes
today
on my open window at dawn—
not because
I wanted to shut You out—
but when You passed by the window,
Your Glory was so bright
I could only soak in Your Love
through the parchment
of my skin.

RIPENESS

With the clouds
hung
like alabaster pears
in the late night
sky—
polished
and
translucent,
I breathed
Luminescence.

And my body
evaporated.

INTO PYREX
_____

You poured Your hot liquid
into me—I broke
and pieces scattered.

Gathering up shards by hand,
You held me in Your crucible
until I melted,
pouring my new form.

I cannot sit in a cupboard—
be displayed on a shelf.
I cannot hold keys, coins,
or others' sundries.

Shatter me again.

The crucible and hand,
Your Glass-blower's spin,
and the press of the heat—
from the depth of Your body—
render me pure.

Julian Lynn

VIBRANT

_____

The sun came down
this afternoon,
splitting through
the layers
of gritty film
and fog
draped
around my senses.

Colors vibrated.
Edges crisped.
And objects became
see-through.

Atomic.

Fragile mind,
do not attempt to hold
this virgin fruit.

UTTERANCE
_____

What I have not articulated

is my gratitude

for the day.

It has been wild

and tame,

pleasant

and sour.

I hold it in my mouth.

APPENDIX

After selecting the verse for *Divine Fruit*, I felt that the volume was incomplete without the inclusion of a selection of practices or methods. The appendix provides inquisitive, disciplined readers with a sampling of practices which may foster introspection, awareness and internal stillness. As with any new venture, please exercise prudence and listen to the wisdom of your own body when sampling these methods. If you find that a practice is not serving you, discontinue its use. Also, if you suffer chronic health concerns, please consult a physician before embarking on a new regimen.

Walking Breath

Many breath-based practices require us to carve out seated quiet time during the day. This practice is excellent for those with active lives because it is a moving practice, designed to be enjoyed while walking solo down a street or running an errand on foot to the neighborhood store.

As you begin walking, open with a comfortable exhalation to cleanse your system. Then, slowly begin inhaling while counting your steps. Establish an initial inhalation lasting just four to seven steps. Remember to be very gentle with your lungs. Everything should feel comfortable and relaxed. Next, exhale to the same number of steps.

After several minutes of enjoying your even breathing pattern, you may choose to add an extra step or two to both your inhalation and exhalation. Continue to honor your body's unique lung capacity.

Bending and stooping are contraindicated for this practice. Enjoy this practice while walking solely upright. Discontinue this practice should you experience discomfort. Your breathing should be fluid, comfortable and easy.

Sunlight Meditation

On a bed, stack three pillows behind you with your neck supported. Your torso is propped comfortably at a gentle, forty-five degree angle. Next, place a pillow under each forearm or under your armpits. The last two pillows rest individually under each gently bent knee. Think about melting into the hammock of space you have created for yourself and relax your eye lids.

Focus on and even your breathing. Draw your attention into your body, begin saying internally, "I feel the sunlight on my toes." Then, "I feel sunlight warming my feet." Next, "I feel sunlight permeating my ankles." Continue moving up the body, noting each body part by name. When you reach the torso, work through the torso naming at least three sections: the pelvic region, midriff and chest. Follow by moving down the arms, finally coming back to the shoulders, neck and head.

You may also decide to begin with sunlight warming the crown of your head and by naming the unique organs of your head and, then, working your way down through the neck and onto the remainder of your body.

Resonance

In a space where you feel comfortably singing, come to a tall, seated position on the front edge of a chair. (For best results, be sure to clear your nose completely first.) Draw your palms together with your fingers facing the sky and spread your fingers apart. Plant the outside edges of your thumbs on the center of the sternum. Close your eyes. Exhale completely through your nose. Inhale completely through your nose and then on your next exhaling breath, sing the long letter "A" out through your mouth, using a single tone. You should feel your breastbone gently vibrating under your thumbs.

Continue through a list of long vowels, trying new notes as you go. (You may use the long vowel sounds from English to practice: "A" as in mate, "E" as in meet, "I" as in might, "O" as in moat, "U" as in mute—or—"OO" as in moot.) Find the note or tone that best suits your heart on a given day. You will experience a resonance in the whole of your body when you find the right tone. Cycle through the complete list of vowels three times, utilizing this tone. (Note: English-language sonorants [*e.g.* "L," "M," and "N"] may also be employed.)

The Golden Ball

While reclining with your spine straight, envision a gold ball, approximately two-and-one-quarter inches in diameter, floating inside the front of your body below your navel. Using your inhaling breath, heat the ball from a warm yellow to a glowing orange until the ball becomes red hot. If you have never worked with the breath before, this may be enough to practice.

Once you have successfully heated the ball to a glowing red, you may begin traveling with the ball inside of your torso. Drop the ball from below the navel to the pelvic floor, resting there until you experience a shift in your breathing—from jagged to smooth or heavy to light. Determine whether or not your ball is still red hot. Pause to reheat the ball on your inhalations. Travel with the ball to the inside of the sacrum. Rest here and at each vertebra up the spine while monitoring the ball and the breath. Next, travel inside of the skull and allow the ball to drop out of the nose. Catch the ball on the extended tongue and swallow three times, taking the ball into your throat. Then, travel with the ball to the inside of the sternum before allowing it to drop from the tip of the sternum back into position just below the navel. Rest for a moment.

Divine Fruit

Spring Leaf

Come to a comfortable reclining position, or sit tall at the front half of a firm chair. Draw your attention to the center point of your brow. Visualize a small, bright-green bud at the center point of your forehead. The sun—in your mind's eye—is overhead. Your view is clear and your focus singular. Notice the tender quality of the curled leaf. Under the warm influence of the sun, the leaf begins to open. Notice how small the leaf is, even as it is opening.

Now, as the sun shifts position, in the mind's sky, light comes to rest behind the leaf. The luminescent quality of the bright-green leaf becomes even more pronounced. The delicate leaf is fully open and sunlight plays off the leaf's edges, seeming to wink and sparkle. As you observe the sunlight shining directly through the leaf, notice how bright the leaf has become.

Over the course of a day, when you are not actively engaged in another obligation, such as driving or another activity which requires your full attention, return to the bright-green leaf in your mind's eye and note the calming effect this practice may produce in your body.

INDEX

1,000 Blossoms	....	7
A Letter from the Sun	....	49
Appendix	....	59
As Lichens	....	46
Asunder	....	10
Calling Cards	....	39
Chant	....	20
Daily Bread	....	45
Desire	....	24
Divine Fruit	....	1
Elegant and Concise	....	30
Endless	....	23

Essential Self	....	32
Falling	....	48
Flow	....	21
Fool	....	15
Full	....	18
Gifts	....	16
Grace	....	72
Grammar	....	31
Hearts	....	47
Holy Matchstick	....	33
Index	....	65
Into Pyrex	....	54
Know Love	....	6
Liberation	....	17
Meditation	....	5
Midnight Sky	....	41
Most Pleasing	....	36
Nakedness	....	26
New Poem II	....	51
On That Sweet Final Day	....	22
Out Loud	....	2
Parchment	....	52
Pine Cone	....	25

Plastic and Red Hot...	....	35
Progress	....	28
Promise	....	40
Quiet	....	3
Rabid	....	27
Rank	....	8
Remaining	....	19
Ripeness	....	53
Sacred	....	50
Salt Water	....	34
Seamlessly	....	11
Sidewalks	....	42
Sliced Lemon/Crushed Mint	....	43
Spark of Life	....	14
Spring Green	....	9
Sun Streamers	....	44
Twice More	....	38
Unbridled	....	12
Underbelly	....	13
Utterance	....	56
Vibrant	....	55
While Napping	....	4

Divine Fruit

ACKNOWLEDGMENTS

I would like to acknowledge the support of my immediate family—my mother, spouse and child—without whom I would, quite literally, not be here. You gave selflessly of your time, energy, care and resources to make the process of my return happen. This project and my experiences of Union would not have been possible without you or your own collective willingness and individual abilities to take many additional and sometimes difficult steps along your own spiritual paths. I would also like to acknowledge my heartfelt appreciation to my editor, Maridel Allinder. You provide me with invaluable feedback, sensitive words, thorough notes and the gift of your keen and inquisitive mind. You have my gratitude.

ABOUT THE AUTHOR

Julian Lynn is a student and seeker, who continues to practice, listen and inquire. One of her greatest joys comes from assisting clients through pranic work, in which individuals strive to enhance and expand their experiences of the Self. She wishes for everyone an experience of Union, so that we may all come to know and understand our essential Oneness. You may find her work at www.julianlynn.com.

This book is printed on acid-free paper. Three fonts were used in the creation of this work: Cordia New, Gabriola and Times New Roman. All photographs were executed by the author.

GRACE

───────────────────────────

Turn your face
into
the Light.